# The Magician's Handbook

Poems by

## Grant Clauser

BOOKS

Regional Publishing, National Voice
A division of Philadelphia Stories

Regional Publishing, National Voice
A division of Philadelphia Stories

PS Books
93 Old York Road
Ste. 1-753
Jenkintown, PA 19046
www.psbookspublishing.org

Published by PS Books,
a division of Philadelphia Stories, Inc.
9780990471585

Cover Image: ©2017 bubaone
Cover & Book Design: Andrew Whitehead

# CONTENTS

# Magic in Theory and Practice

We buy our life
*as is*
and try to fix it.

It's best to believe everything
at once
while moving toward the door
with the easiest escape.

The real magic
is that we choose
a card
knowing all the time
it's a trick.

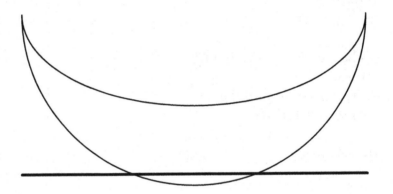

# Part 1:
# Neophyte

# The Good Lie

(after Tracy K Smith)

When some people talk about god
they speak as if it were an astonishing sunset,
something they'd understand better
if only they'd paid attention
in middle school science class.
It looms like disaster over fields,
slips behind the hills where maybe
their parents live or the Walmart went up
a few years ago and drove the small stores
out of town. And soon
the sun vanishes into the trees
leaving behind it the great expectation
of stars, a residual light
the way the tide leaves small pools
along the shore where life began.
When I was small I learned to burn
ants and worms with a magnifying glass
under the sun's sharp attention.
Let me tell you something—
every sunset is a promise
the way seasons and tulips
and volcanoes are promises,
all things we keep alive in memory
out of fear that when we open our eyes
in the blue yawn, it will all be true
or it won't.

# The Magician Welcomes his Audience

The first audience is always family,
living room arranged
around the coffee table
and a Mickey Mouse Magic kit
hidden behind the La-Z-Boy.

Handkerchiefs produce silk flowers.
Three balanced balls become two,
become one, then melt into the darkness
of a palm, a pocket.

Years later counting the eyes
in a night club, a fire hall,
the late-night train ride home—
he learns to study the difference
between paying attention
and scrutiny—

the ones who want to see through
the darkness are the enemy.
The others, for whom darkness
is the comfort of sleep, something
you trust to hold you through silence
and doubt—
those are like his interchangeable pigeons
all cooing the same infuriating note.

# Lights in the Cornfield

The night my father saw lights
hovering over a cornfield,
I was just a baby and he
20-something, trim
and back from the reserves,
a new job kept him up
late at night, away from home,
dinners usually a sandwich
wrapped in wax paper,
always ham and provolone,
dark mustard and ice tea,
and he must have driven that road
a 100 times before
until the night he saw lights
hovering over the cornfield,
a dozen of them, he says,
rising and falling in a pattern
not making any sound or sense
or moving closer
until he slammed the car door
and took a step,
colors waiting in the dark distance,
just one more step until his foot
would touch the course field,
the same one I collected quartz
from 10 years later, looking
for signs of light having been there,
leaving something for us to hold,
but he turned back,
closed the door on the blue Pontiac
and drove home
to other lights still waiting,
where my mother had started
to warm the coffee,
familiar sounds of the room.

# Stalker

All the neighborhood mothers
locked their kids indoors at night,
the summer they found Rose's body
in the woods behind the park house.

Faces pressed to window screens,
we heard bullfrogs test
their throats against lighting bugs
as Perseids streaked across the sky.

We imagined comic book perverts
prowling alleys, trench coats
and pockets full of candy
packed to lure the girls away.

We imagined ninjas, stalkers,
horror movie killers with hockey masks
pulled over twisted faces,
over-sexed always the first victims.

We teased Shelly near to tears
that she was next in line, breasts
as big as older girls, that kiss
from Robert as good as Judas' kiss.

Until cops caught the real killer,
sitting at home alone,
news stories of his daughter's case
in the paper on the floor.

Released at last, we hit the woods
that night, caught catfish in the creek,
filled jars with fireflies, our heads
still full of stalkers and Shelly undressing in the dark.

# The Magician in High School

He never considered fitting in,
but disappearing was something
to shoot for.

Memorizing every corner
in the school building,
which doors locked
and which didn't,
took an entire year.

By then he was nearly
invisible already

except for the sound he made
in the back of the room
when Cindy leaned her hip
against the Spanish teacher's desk.

God, but he wanted
to saw that girl in half.

# The History of Magic Part 1

Of course first was fire.
they carried it from
camp to camp
scaring and bewildering the children
who grew so fond of it
they gave it new names.
One day as they carried the body
of an elder out to a field
one of the children
remembered the fire.
How it danced and made the skin move,
so he fetched it
and touched it
to the old man's body
and in that moment
invented god.

# Bushkill Creek Amusement Park

I remember most the mud
after the flood of '78 that kicked
the Haunted House forever to a tilt

and then the one in '85 that rose
the roller rink off the ground
and rafted it down the rushing creek.

For years the Wild Mouse hung stuck
halfway up the second climb
while the calliope banged a broken melody

on the carousel you loved, the brass ring
always too high to reach, mustangs
chipped and fading in the heat.

I miss the wooden slide and barrel ride,
just the simple thrills that filled
our throats, rode the failing

light to early evening when couples
snuck behind the snack stand
to feel their way around their youth.

I think again of roller skates scratching
rough over warped boards, Mable selling tickets
to the Tilt-a-Hurl and how the creek looked

from the top of the Salt and Pepper
Shaker, ringing the park like a snake,
and then the drop, always the surprise we'd fake.

# Between Two Fortune Tellers at the Midway

You can only have one
future no matter how
indecisive you are.

Outstretched palm, crystal ball or tarot.
Runes that spell disaster,
love or money all come back

to how much you want it,
what you're willing to try.
The woman on your arm wants

cotton candy, a drink to quench
the midway's traveled dust.
You hear gypsies in the curtains,

incense drifting past the hot dog stand's
greasy fog, a chance to see
where all this goes

because inside each of us
there's a map of things
we've lost, signs we missed

or misread along the long way
from home, so now a new direction
in competing divinations.

Here among the carnival's
bump and shuffle crowd
may be the answer

in a deck of cards,
the way fortune surely waits
for someone in a 7-11 lottery ticket,

if you could choose
the right mystic, the one who's been waiting
all her life for only you.

# Slender Man

Of course it's hard to accept
that the girl raised
from squalling pluck
through middle school's
energized bounce
could be the same one
they talk about on TV.
Girl who baited the trap.
Tied her schoolmate's
hands behind her back
before stabbing her 20 times.
They were friends since 4th grade
and we know how hard
loyalty is. Lunch table politics,
the Instagram intimidations
that sort the young
into seed packets, labels
that dig their way in.
But that's a hard line
to cross. It's a rare crack
that turns to a canyon.
Who's to say there wasn't
a voice in the shadow,
a hand to guide the plan,
the host of it all,
not like a party
but a disease.

# A Tarot Reading

She turns over the Knight of Wands,
you breathe, she pauses
to count the swords on the next card,
note the direction
a horse faces in death,
how its eyes follow her hand
as she taps the table

and talks about the circumstances
of love, work, money.
The Page of Pentacles has mother issues.
In the Nine of Swords a man
cradles his face in his hands,
and she warns you about regret,
how it leads to The Hermit's trail.

On the way home, rain slicks
the sidewalks, polishes the leaves
on trees. All promises are temporary
based on context. Will the Hanged Man
eventually stop swinging or
turn his face to you and smile?

# Nova

*This car's still good,*
I tell the mechanic.
*Please do what you can.*
And as he explains
how much it will cost,
how there's no guarantee it will last,
I'm thinking of the Ohio winter
we tried to push it out
of a ditch, snow
filling gaps in my sleeves and hood
and you revving the engine—
the only sound we heard that night
as snowflakes filled every
space in my vision, the weight
of the car sliding back down
the bank, the heater failing
as white and dark closed
in around us.
How we tried everything,
tow and chain and stones
wedged under the tires
until finally we gave in,
caught a ride back to town
and slept late into the next day
trying to forget our stuck car.
And we made love that morning
like an eclipse,
or two far away lights
coming together in a crash
that would blind you
if you looked head on.

# Graduating from Magician School

This isn't the first day
of the rest of your life,
the commencement speaker said.
That was yesterday
and you missed it.

The adepts glare
at each other in their borrowed
graduation robes.

When they throw up their caps
the sky turns
into a flock of startled doves.

# Darwinian

It took millennia for cave fish
to finally lose their eyes,
like light bulbs failing
in an empty room.

Here, as the woods grow dim
my eyes adjust to see through dark,
hands turned callused
from swinging my father's axe.

This is how we meet the world,
bend our lives around the things
we hold close, dress in layers
when the wind is cold.

At some point we all need
to evolve like animals, crawl
from water into air and leave
another skin behind,

but skins have their own
lives, vestiges of love
and scars we try to hide, eyes
still bright behind our cloudy lids,

and when you bring the cave fish
into light, it only takes a generation
for old habits to return,
startled pupils moving under skin.

# Falling in Love with a Fiji Mermaid

*Fiji mermaids were common gaffs at carnival sideshows. They were usually made by combining the head and torso of a monkey with the tail of a fish.*

It's easy to confuse lies
for love,
believe that the palm reader
wasn't out to pick your pocket.
We're held together
by weak filaments
like the stitches
buried at the equator
of fish scale and monkey waist.
It's the eyes too,
stitched shut,
nothing to look into or out of,
closed skin, dried
to the touch.
It's cheap to dream
of such things,
coral meadows where
bull sharks menace
mermaids to their caves.
Where Fiji women toss
their stillborn babies to the sea
and they come back
remade by waves.
But in the end
the carney calls you
back to the midway light.
No time left for fantasy.
The Fiji mermaid's tail
is cracked and spitting straw.
You see the stitches now
exposed for what they are—

threads that hold
two bodies together
but cannot make a whole.

# Sideshow Freaks at Lemon's Tavern

Her red hair shone with hay bale light,
the bearded lady from the midway fair
and with her stood the geek with nails
half up his nose, left from the night's
last show, where I paid to see the pale
dead twins in jars, the mummy's hand
and artifacts who's stories fail
to tell the truth, that Grady Stiles
was not a lobster, but a killer
who's unfinished hands shot the man
who planned to marry Grady's daughter
and got away, here drinking beer
with college girls who shivered at the sight
of Lobster Boy leaning at the bar that night.

*(Grady Stiles, known as Lobster Boy, confessed to murder in 1978, but only served a 15 year probation term and was himself murdered in 1992. He was born with the condition ectrodactyly.)*

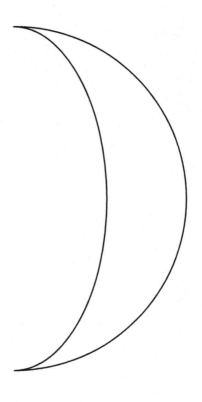

# Part 2
# Adept

# The Magician's Opening Act

They compete for the same
audience, the same piece of stage,
juggler and magician,

but there's no denying
the appeal of danger with grace—
seven axes in the air
while spitting fire
at your fans,

while he sits backstage
sorting cards,
trying to ensure the notches
all face right,

whispering sweetly
to the doves
about risk
and reward.

# Midway to the End of the World

Between the Tempest and the Globe of Death,
the midway's famous oddities parked
along the fairground's muddy
riverside where a hundred year
flood sweeps every fifty years
just to keep us sharp.

There in a cage painted
to look real the geek
chewed on broken glass
and flashed his meat-hooked nipples
at every pretty girl who passed
within his reach and the too sweet
smell of sick puddles at his feet.

Each college jock dumb enough
to dare his glance got spat on
when they turned away to laugh.

You know this as the moment
the world ran down, but kept going.
The Lazarus lie that man can go
so far and come back whole or same.
Like movie zombies, walking
but for want of brains.

It doesn't matter if the geek
is an act or just what's left over
after drugs or damaged genes
made this mass of self hate and storm.
We'll buy the story, ride the Ferris Wheel
and lose the midway games
till dark and end the night
in our own zombie stupor,
watching bikers hurl themselves in circles
till one or all end up in flames.

# How the Magician Met His Wife

He knew she was the one
the way he knew a king of hearts
was in the left breast pocket of her jacket.

The difference between swept away
and swept off your feet
is like knowing something's a trick
but not knowing how it's done.

Hypnotism is best practiced
at bars after last call
when everyone looks around
to see who's still standing
and why they're staring at you.

# Kabir Says

*"Brother, I have seen some amazing things"*

I've never tasted fresh organic honey
or been to the Mall of America (a lie, I have)
or attended the live taping
of a late-night TV show (OK, another lie).

In a pork factory in Pennsylvania
workers play the sounds of fireworks and cannons
on the slaughterhouse floor
because fear is a flavor you can taste
when glands release it in the meat.

I'm afraid of roller coasters
because in 1972 five children were crushed
on the Big Dipper in Wandsworth England.

Kabir saw fish in treetops
and lions protecting cattle
from the night's evil,
but mostly I stare at this desk
thinking of things to say.

I've seen the Forbidden City,
which isn't forbidden
if you have a ticket
and I shared that moment
with 1,500 other tourists,
mostly children in school uniforms
that make them look like cartoons
or what I believe cartoons
would look like if they came to life.

By now you've realized I have nothing
to say, and I've taken about four minutes
to do that.

Kabir said there's a moon in the body,
but we cannot see it.
Sometimes at night I listen
for the cicadas to stop
like the moment of silence
when we flip a record,
and when they start again
you realize how surrounded
you are, the darkness dense
with their mouths,
their wings sawing
like violin bows
on femurs.

If there's a moon in the body
it must be the heart,
never the same light twice
like the river Heraclitus
got caught in between flood
and drought.
Every night a different moon,
a new face staring back
from an auditorium of stars.

When the moon sets
and the lions finally tire
and consume the cows,
then all of our works
truly are zero.

# Field Guide to the Suburbs

If raccoons invade your chimney
don't light a fire
or they'll race like flaming cannonballs
around your house
and burn it to the ground.

Snakes under the foundation
must be killed before spring mating
or their orphaned eggs will rot
and rise through floorboards.

Bees too will smell like bitter
honey in the walls
when the old queen dies, and no one
tells the workers when to feed.

Everything out there is coming
for you, the eyes in the trees
are buzzards, and bats curve
their sonar toward your hair.

Tell yourself to breathe—
moonlight shining in the yard
ignites the eyes of skunks
gorging through your garbage,
deer gnawing on your shrubs.

That feeling you have is real.
All the pets are off their leashes.
Blind voles tunnel under your feet,
looking for the light they lost.

# The Magician Practices Sword Swallowing

By this stage in life
he'd swallowed a lot,
but gives the audience
what they want—danger
and a little blood.

As with most important lessons,
understanding the trick
and sliding the steel
down your throat
are two different things.

Start small, a butter knife
or broken switch blade
until you advance to screwdrivers
up the nose.

The more you want, he tells himself,
the farther you'll go
until one day you feel
the cold blade slip
past your heart.

With each beat
the edge chips a tooth.

# Van Gogh's Sunflowers

Van Gogh's yellow sunflowers
are turning toad brown
because the lead in them
can't stand the light.

On the first day of spring
I think of gardens,
the insistence of tiny seeds
to spread their palms
across the earth.

Before he stepped with pistol
into that field of poppies,
Van Gogh's yellow-stained fingers
cupped his head, held
his own hands, hot and cold.

Decay always begins
at the root of things, paint
drying on the brush,
the fission of neutrons
into a night bursting
with colors.

The day always comes
when every sunrise
is a warning from the dark,
and every kiss
is a kiss goodbye.

So the things that kill us best,
kill us slowly,
roots pushing their fingers
through humus and rock,
foundations failing and crumbling.

# For You, My Love, Alchemy

Let's begin with definitions—
Earth, the rooms we rearrange
to fit our belongings.
Fire, the look we give to things
we want.

Take this gold ring.
Its weight and emptiness a mystery
of being and not,
the difference between
a spoken word and a whisper.

This house after a winter
of heavy snow emerges
one morning like a time machine
returned after a long trip.

The children we left
to their business
are grown and difficult
to recognize.

Take this metal
and drop it in the ocean.
All the sea aches
to watch it rust.

Take this stone
and crush it into sand.
Entire lives are lived
on such beaches.

# At the Occult Flea Market and Used Book Emporium

Every bargain is deceiving—
> the cost of trinkets hidden in the fingerprints

> > of those who held them last, pins abandoned in the
> > second-hand voodoo doll
> > > the way comets leave a trail of shrapnel
> > > suspended in their wake

> > or Spock, exposed to radiation
> > > in the *Wrath of Khan*
> > > > can't touch his friend goodbye

# The Magician Buys a Lottery Ticket

This should be easy.
He holds his dollar to his forehead
and thinks of a number

but all he gets
is the backwash of last night's
dream, random colors,

his daughter's birthday,
which he realizes
he forgot again.

# Zombie

In every zombie movie someone
will make a choice between love
and life, between bringing the ax
down into the forehead of family,
a father, a young wife or younger
brother, or accepting that fate meant
them to be food for someone else,
that the mouth they know as well
as their own hands will swallow
them, bite by animal bite, dead eyes
rolling back in their head with rapture
and that's the moment
in a struggle that looks like an embrace
when both lose their grip on the world
with fingers clawed or manicured,
eyes weeping or drained of light,
the choice to fight the reaching arms
or to succumb to love's hunger
that what life was is no more,
that opening a beating heart
with bare hands, or opening your
heart to others, is the same, a rending
of reality, where this world
once bright with cars and laughter,
now a sundown slaughter, and we
the audience to such profound
carnage have to wonder, would
I crush his or her skull and so survive
or would I make the choice
that love, no matter how savage,
is still a kind of love, and with it
watch the sun rise over our world
changed, together, but falling apart?

# More Advice for My Daughters

Maybe the moon doesn't shadow
us across the field and into
the pine pitch black of woods,
but when we come out again
it's waiting like a reliable horse.

Tonight the moon went alone
into the clouds and eclipsed
a star we couldn't follow.
Some business in the night is solo.

So know that you, my morning stars,
can't go far without me.
Our tides are closed to change
even as waves wash out our
footprints in the sand.

The sky you want and the sea
you have are two parts of a whole.
Know that waves go on forever,
as they circle round the world.

Embrace the grace lunations
of the nights, the grip they have
and their steady light. Your moon
is bright as feathers floating
on the waves, the piece we save.

# The Magician Turns 40

Every time he pulls a penny
from the ear of a child
or pops a balloon to reveal
the intact egg he'd smashed
a minute before,
there's a quaking
in his knees,
the matrix of cell and bone
that holds him up believes
the fall is coming—
that an enthusiastic parent
will pat him too hard on the back
and shake loose
every handkerchief and card,
every dove and throwing knife,
and he'll be caught naked
like a tree in winter,
leaves scattered down the road,
bark peeling back in the snow.

# Ouija

We can't bypass the pleasantries of speech
and expect the trust that hands convey
touching and turning, feeling our way
around the evening, our mystery or

just something misheard, a figure
on the wall, a shadow or figure
of speech. You pushed left, me
right, and in turn we guide our

view of things, the yes and no
of ambiguity, the evening made of glass
and paper, the tension between touching
hands and touching empty space, erased.

# The Magician at Airport Security

He empties his pockets
into the tray—
skeleton keys, double-sided coins,
a pinch of sparkle dust

that gets more attention
from the sentries
than the razor hidden
in his sleeve
for cutting rope.

When the dust leaves
his finger, a thought cloud
of smoke bursts
like a chewing gum bubble
and four men draw
their tasers

while he steps unnoticed
from the other side
of the X-ray booth
jingling coins in his pocket.

# Séance

Because circles are infinite
we hold hands, let the want
of our bodies rise around us
like mayflies rising from a river.
Because voices are made of waves
that travel space until they break
up against a dam, we ask for signs
that prove the world isn't flat
where ships tumble and never return.
Because once, at a train station
there was a face in the crowd
that looked like you, and her eyes
reflected light the way
a beaver pond holds the whole sky
in its mountain gaze.
Because I wanted to reach out,
touch the water and your hand
but my grip was weak,
the promise of voices rising
over the heads of the crowd
until even the sky wasn't enough
to hold it all, like oceans
forcing themselves beyond the beach
to take what doesn't belong
to the sea.
So here we are, dragging
your name across the dark
bank of the room,
sifting through Styx's flotsam
for a whisper, a wind
something to make it rain.

# The Magician's Yard Sale

You never know what you'll find
because crates empty and fill
of their own accord.

Tablecloths stand without tables
while an umbrella holder
loaded with swords
seems to rattle
with rage.

Everything's a bargain,
two for one, the dimensions
are hard to calculate
so just make an offer.

You can learn a lot
about people
from the stuff they sell
for change.

When your quarter
disappears in his palm
you'll probably find it later
tucked behind your ear.

# Suburban Grimoire

Your father passed it to you
just as his father passed it to him.
How to tie a necktie straight,
the proper use of levels
and ways to bleed a radiator quiet—
always the right tool for the job,
wards against winter, insulation
and the invocations that weather
demands, like chopping wood
to release the dryads, mowing
the lawn as defense against
the dark stares of demons.
Equilibrium for the magus
comes in balancing the checkbook.
Conjuring takes practice,
chalk circles, pentagrams,
the right recipe for chili
and nine layers of hell nachos
for Sunday.
Some rites are forgotten,
others best left untouched,
but the 9-to-5 incantations,
the daily rituals of boredom
command respect, deference
to the damned that went before,
the keepers of secrets,
grand masters of tax breaks,
hidden art of used car negotiations,
charms to keep the furnace running
are precious to hold, like a chalice,
a seven pointed garden rake, the claws
of a spell-bound devil
we call a heart that eventually
eats its own way out.

# The Magician Pays His Bills

Electronic funds transfer
he thinks, is like the Bill in the Lemon
trick
and the bank is the lemon.

If only he knew more
about fruit
like how Chris Angel is able
to drop a watermelon
from a 50-foot crane
and pull a live rabbit
from the smashed pink pulp.

Now that's a money trick
he thinks, calculating the cost
of renting a crane,
cleanup for the failed attempts.

That's the thing about failures,
a cost/risk equation
of fruit and blood.

When he licks
the mortgage envelop
the glue tastes
like lemon.

# Ode to a Jackalope

Like Sasquatch or the Tooth Fairy
everyone believed in it at one time,
at least a little, how evolution
or mutation could maybe, really,
have made such a thing.
We know stranger beasts exist—
Narwhal, platypus, two-headed snakes
and the Venus flytrap—all monsters
you can prove with books
and not half as likely
as a jackalope's pointed rack.
Even the sky we wander under,
the one we watch late summer nights,
has stars for every mystery we can name
yet in between each spectral light
are holes even dreams can't reach.
At the Buckhorn Diner one mounted head
grazed above the cash register
for 50 years like a story told
so many times it becomes legend
until fire burned the restaurant down.
What if that was the last
of its kind? Gone to ash
in grease fire splendor
till just the glass eyes remained.
Like Chupacabra chasing down
calves in Texas dawns,
or the Jersey Devil spreading
its bitter wings across the Pine Barrens,
Jackalope is the door we step through,
the name we give to small nightmares
or delights, the hope we place in stars
that mysteries are real, that fire spreads

spontaneously like spring weeds
in an empty field, and nature's twisted
means to an end has to take some risks
to make a life worth living,
even if it turns out to be a lie.

# Naming the Hurricanes

Ten percent of the choice
is just the luck of the alphabet.
J comes after I then K.
Next we move to mothers in law,
black sheep brother or drunk uncles.
What about girls
who dumped you in high school?
Who gets to flatten sand dunes?
Who gets to strand the elderly on rooftops
while dogs float down streets
on billboards? Someone must
have hated a certain Sandy
Feared a certain Andrew
to pin them forever to destruction.
Why not name the spring rain
we fall in love to at the windowsill?
The sun shower we splashed through
in flip flops at the beach?
Who do we call the first snow
of December? The one we wished
would come and hope it stays all month,
a prize we earned for November's gray?
I want to name this bright day
after you. Call it daughter
for the way it rose sleepy
in the morning then warm
on my arms in the yard.
Every wind becomes someone
we once friended.
Everything that falls from the sky
should be someone we loved
and need to go on touching.

# The Magician's Vacation

There's no place he can go
where the universe can't
find him.

So much on his mind,
the comings and goings
of stage smoke,
how to read the facial
ticks of a tiger
and the number
of clicks
in his favorite padlock

that he can't relax
even on a beach.
Instead, he counts
sand grains and sea gulls,
listens for the cries
of sailors in a conch shell

and rearranges the stars
to better explain
the weather.

# Search Engine Optimization

All our queries return as snow,
wind piles it against the shed doors,
the driveway sheeted in ice.
Between the pine tree and its scent
is a hemorrhage where blue jays
fight each other over seeds.
A poltergeist of wind scatters
cones across the yard.

We refine our terms, narrow the options
while a neighbor's cat stalks
the bird feeder by the rear shed.
Between the feather and the flight—
long moments of nothing.
He's almost stone, patience
the weight some people carry
on their backs.

Disappearing is easy for wind.
It laughs out of reach even from snow.
Between the snow drift and the night
there's hunger and hope
that what you want to know falls
out of the sky, covers the yard
in white, and all you see
are the footsteps of who was here,
blood and feathers on the ground.

# Magician Sends his Kids to College

Letting go is one of the few things
that comes easy to him.

There's only so much you can trust
to good plans,
but tigers will be tigers
and sometimes bare their teeth.

His daughter is quick to say
goodbye; his son
slouches around the car
with his hands out for cash.

When the magician gets home
to walls serenely silent
he finds the rabbit cages
all shattered on the garage floor,
headless bodies scattered
in the corners.

# Planting the Garden

The thing about work is
there's so much of it,
like mosquitoes in a swamp
or words or hate or those ants pouring
endlessly from their ruptured mound
when I push the tiller through
the ground, one just can't
bear it all.

In these straight and ordered rows,
little hills, I measure with a stick
and push the seedlings deep
I hope enough to root,
to spread and ripen.
We've just one chance
to do this right,
to get that thing to grow.

And then the weeds,
crabgrass or dandelion or thistle,
like a misfit dating your daughter.
There's only so much fight
you can make, before nature,
a horned boy and his flute,
sees fit to piss
on your lettuce.

# Spell To Settle Strife Among Relations

Catch a buzzard by its beak
and break the stones in its knees,

feed the buzzard bones to your uncle
and the wife he beats

and he will love her forever
and follow her about the house

like a scavenger picking up
anything she leaves behind.

# At the Magician's Club

You know the type.
Arguing over who
has the biggest wand
or the fiercest tiger.

The booze is second rate
at best
but no one says so.

The strangest thing
he's learned
is not the secret
to the Mismade Girl,

but how he can
make a living
from birthday parties,
senior centers,
the simple pleasure
of shuffling cards.

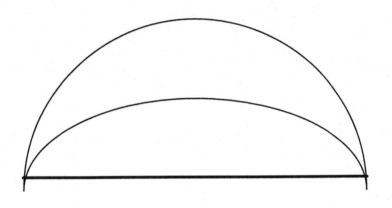

# Part 3
# Magus

# The Magician's Handbook

In the margins he scratches
a note on how to fold a rabbit
into a matchbox
and the best body cavities
for hiding handkerchiefs.

In the back are the names
of every girl
he sawed in half,
small hearts drawn
next to the best.

It's not the lost loves
he regrets most
or the lean years
he ate mostly
balloon animals,

but that he'd spent
so much time
hiding how it's done
that he forgot
how it ends.

# Secrets of the Great Escape Artists

It's not enough that there's a razor hidden
between ass cheeks
or a key held under the tongue.
These padlocks, leather straps
and canvas sleeves can't contain
you if your mind was free
from the start.
You can count on someone
to call for help, for a woman
in the back row to faint
as the clock tick-clicks close to panic time,
bubbles rising from the tank
you thrash in. You can count
on time slowing down, minutes
stretched across your lungs
as the skin of a drum
and then the twang
as time unwraps its fist
and lets you go.
The secret's in the waiting
when all attention's on the last breath
like family holding hands
around a hospital bed,
the audience so sure of your death
that they see it rise up
in front of them
and then you tap it on the shoulder,
remind your death that time flies
and stands still at the same time
and the nick of it is enough
to slip past unnoticed.
Not a cheat so much as a gamble,
that a trap door is always open
if you're willing to step through.

# Answer to Henri Cole's
## *Green Shade*

Even if you could
lay down in the grass
among Nara's semi-wild deer,
if you could get close enough
to look into the nut-brown eyes
and dream of years free from crave
or covet, and believe you wanted
nothing more than green shade
you'd be wrong as the deer crackers
sold to eager tourists,
because sika deer are vicious
and kick when cornered,
like us, thrashing when threatened.
Here the park closes at dusk each day.
Truth, it was raining then.
Teachers shove their students past
the Great Buddha's tarnished feet
and everywhere "Keep off the Grass"
signs in English and Japanese
intrude on the calm.
There's wanting nothing
until there's nothing to want
and the path always leads
back to parking lots
where cars heat up in the cold rain
to take us home, human and hungry.

# Magician Takes Inventory

After the show
it should add up.

A cut for the house.
A cut for the girl.

And something to feed
the wasting tiger and the car.

But the card deck feels light,
and the swords are dull.

Each night the stage shrinks
like... well, you know.

And the straight jacket
straps buried in the trunk

grow a little tighter
squeezing out all his air.

# Vanishing Point

When he passes his hand over the card deck
and all the hearts turn to clubs, you know
it's an illusion, that things don't change that fast
or vanish into nothing, even a flood

leaves a wasteland of mud and garbage behind
to mark its passing, and the best animal trackers
can find a shadow from the lightest bird
still resting on rocks days after it's flown away.

Driving down a road at night, headlights spreading
the gloom aside like a plow, trees and signs appear
only when they enter the car's bright foreshadow
and vanish behind to a point in the crowding dark.

The magician spreads another deck on the table
and asks you to pick a card. All options open
at this point, like the possible that morning brings
when new light fans out over the yard.

There's nothing fair about nighttime, all
it's options hidden out of sight, like card tricks
of the almighty, the deck loaded against imagination,
until a moment someone steps into the light.

And that's all it takes, behind you a bike wheel
spins in the shrinking arrow of your taillights
and all directions converge into one, the stars,
like diamonds, suddenly turned to spades.

# Ghosts

Like fireflies filling
the distant trees with light,
they appear in the calm of evening
leaving traces in the air,
illuminating nothing
but themselves

# Name

Some people collect their ghosts
like souvenirs from places
they've loved and left,
shadows of highways,
the grand canyons of faith
and roadside attractions
where the woman behind
the counter, the one who said
your name when speaking
to someone else, made you turn
and catch your breath
because you thought
you knew that voice
and burned to hear
it new again.

# The Magician's Last Assistant

She was good at vanishing
and rolling her eyes
in mock death each night
after the swords pierced her
like a steak.

He praised her balance,
ability to hold her breath
long enough to bring
the crowd to panic.

But for all the risk she took,
the knives that grazed
her cheek,
she had no stomach
for the stage, the need to wait
behind a curtain
with restraints around her writs.

# Prayer

The kind of prayers we make—
like tennis balls thrown
to blind dogs,
like leaving cat food out
for strays then finding skunks
gathered on the porch.

We can't ask anymore
after the gifts of earth and water,
maybe fire, that you may cup
its heat in your palm,
send the dark back into corners.

Prayers don't work that way.
What we've come to expect
is more wind rattling
the rain gutters loose,
the dog house roof rotting
and falling to the ground.

Let's make a prayer
for stomachs, that they
may cease their anxious knots,
that tense shoulders soften
and migraines fade,
that skunks continue to prowl
around the back porch
but all you notice
are the wild flowers
they left untouched
in the garden.

# The Bats of Evansburg

The story goes
that a small Lenape boy
followed the bats
one morning into a hollow
under a sycamore tree
and came out three days later
and a mile away.
All he ever said
about his days in the cave
was that the walls whispered
things that must be a tongue
only the dead know.
Now 200 years later
the bats of Evansburg are gone
and nobody talks to the dead.

# The Magician Dreams

Every cause has its effect.
The moon crawling on all fours
leading a pack of mangy dogs.
A man alone in his house
breeding homunculi in jars.

It's the doom of mirrors
that they can't turn away.
Every glance ahead is just
a false goodbye. He covers them
with cloth to keep the eyes outside.

Outside, rain without clouds.
Fish fall from the sky like a wish
shot down for wishing wild.
His shadow moves in circles
on the floor, finally settles down
and sleeps some more.

# Poltergeist

To come back from the dead
as a wobbly lamp fixture
or a butter dish sliding
to the floor
may be anticlimactic,
but think of the power
of suggestion—fear
does more damage
than pain in the long run,
potential energy can keep us
lying awake in bed
while kinetic merely shakes it
for a few frantic seconds.

It doesn't work for the living
though—to *want* is stronger,
but not more satisfying than to *have*,
like two lovers searching
for hands in the dark.
I touch a candle flame
and learn its bite
but hold on anyway
despite the burn
it leaves, the flesh
it takes in exchange
for a taste
of its light.

# The Magician's Doves

*They're real,*
he always feels compelled
to say, though children
believe implicitly.

The pearl white feathers
come from decades
of interbreeding
so their wings
are too stunted
to fly.

Of all the animals,
he hates
the doves most

because no matter
how many he crushes
under squares of red satin

they die unsurprised
with their black eyes
always open
as if they knew
the trick
and didn't care.

# The Knowable World

A family in Maine keeps goats that hop all day
with joy. Videos of them dancing
in a pasture spread like clover across
the internet—but what if leaping isn't
a form of delight? What can we know
about the felicity of goats?

Their dance from trough to stump
to the backs of fellow goats
may be nature's response to fear,
like a child who pulls out her own hair
or a mother who poisons her infant
because her mind can't hold itself still.

Maybe tulips blooming in spring
aren't a sign of hope or the summer
sun to come, but the flower's way
of expelling toxins from its body,
a botanical primal scream that all this
will be repeated as the green leaves pray.

Is that the choice we make between faith
and the knowable world, the names
we give to things we love, the things
we turn away from when the brightness fades?
When Eve offered Adam the apple,
she called it a gift, and he gladly accepted
because who would believe what would happen.

# Ode to Bats

*Bats eat a lot of bugs — up to two-thirds of their body weight in insects daily for some species. There's an unexpected side effect of all that insect eating, though. Bat scat is described as "sparkling with insect exoskeletons."—from* Wired

Let's say you follow the rules,
believe in the power of eyes
and hands to know.
That tree roots keep the earth
from blowing into the sea
and trade winds keep the sea
moving in patterns satellites
can track from space.
We're bound by things
we can't see or change
like gravity holding us prisoner
to sea and sand alike.
And yet we live under a sky
with the miracle of bats—
bird and mouse in one skin,
blind and able break rules
to see the smallest flutter
of mosquitoes.
All rules are written
in treachery or fear.
Sometimes even gravity
gets it wrong—the magic
when a mammal first lifts
its body into the sky.
What if we all learned
our own private escape velocity?
The force it takes to change
our lives, to rise
above meager imagination's bounds—
would we risk it?

What holds an animal
aloft more than trust?
Can a blind bat know
that red is the color
of a mosquito's blood
by taste alone?
This evening I trust
the bats above me
will keep their distance,
that satellites circling the earth
are far enough away to not
believe in me, and here even
the mosquito trying desperately
to drain my arm's abundance of blood
holds mysteries I will never understand.
I could say this makes us human,
that the space between us
and the bat is as wide as the
vast sky that separates our lives—
Bats have no room in their hearts
for gravity, hanging upside down
by day from the rotting rafters
of my backyard shed, floor
littered with the insect sparkle
of their waste. The night
fills with echo frequencies
carving our bodies out in space.
If we could see the bat's voice
it would be a web stretching
across the sky like a mad interstate
lit up at night by merging headlights,
all the world's dark places
opened up to us.

# The Magician Turns 60

He's sure someone
in the audience
is snoring—

a deep soft rasp
like pulling a long snake
out of a rabbit hole.

He fears for the rabbit,
but it's probably too late.

The snake's digestive juices
are already breaking down
bone and fur
into liquid nutrients
that will only let the snake
grow stronger.

# it

It gets heavier every year,
weight shifting from shoulder
to shoulder like a poorly packed
rucksack carried too far,
watching the sun advance
across the road
the way a corpse
drags itself out of a grave
in a George Romero movie.

# Idiot's Guide to the Afterlife

The air in purgatory stings
of bar smoke and bleach.
There's broken glass on the floor,
and the band sounds like crickets
sawing through the after-
silence of battlefields.
Every street sign is pimpled
by buckshot, every furry thing
in the shadows turns rabid
and bares its teeth.
Bonfires of old birthday cards
line the road to an outhouse.
Here all your exes are loving
someone else in front of you.
Your best dog dies again
and again in your arms.
The boy you picked on
in seventh grade gym
smokes a Cuban cigar
and flicks the ash in your face.
Every kitchen smell
on your street,
every voice leaking
from window screens,
is a paper cut salted
on your palm.
You stand at the entrance
to a toll booth
where what you owe
is subtracted
from what you've done,
and you know there aren't
enough fingers on your hands
to count off your regrets
to the ferryman.

# A Good Remedy for the Fever by
## *A Long Lost Friend*

She said to draw some blood
and find a young dog to swallow it

Scrape food from the four corners
of your table
and feed it to him in the morning

She said sometimes if you speak
the words cut from trees
before the sun has risen
no one of your family
will ever be bitten by snakes

take the eye of the dog
if a wolf can't be found
and sew it into your right sleeve

this cools the blood by morning
like a noose lightly around
your neck

# Omens and Portents

The cicadas are back
as they promised, murmuring
into the evening from tree trunks
and old fence posts by the pond,
the white noise hum
of the earth's radio.

Here dragonflies dip
their tails, leaving eggs
to hug the pond's meniscus
—summer's first kiss parting
in the June-bug moonlight,
a firefly show rising from tall grass.

The magician reads mystery novels
by lamplight, dozing under
the deep-sea dark of stars.
Wind stirs the trees
like the memories of mistakes
he made, turning faces
away from the breeze.

He measures the night by pages
under the patio's candescent globe.
Like cicadas waiting seventeen years
to chew the green hibiscus, bodies
have their own memories, each
finger, each corpuscled eyelid
closing against constellations.

When you take away the insect
buzz, the night's white fodder,
there's only darkness
and the promises we fill it with,
waiting for earth's warm cradle,
the pleasure of settling into silence,
a dull and finite winding.

# Prodigal Satellite

Eventually even the things
we've launched into space
return to us as flame.

Orbiting the earth like coyotes
around a campsite, the scouts
we launch come slouching

home, their histories lost
in long forgotten contrails,
arms outstretched for warmth

as the link between battery
and perpetual motion finally dies.
There's always an atmosphere

to break through, a river or border
to cross, a burn upon reentry.
Those words you wrote on the wall

before you left are still there
covered by paint, now
someone else's space.

# The Devil You Know

What if you were pulled over
one night? The road is quiet.
You know you were speeding—
someplace important to go
but the cop looks tired and almost
lets you off.

He asks to look in the trunk
and you tell him it's only the Devil
bound, gagged and kicking
cloven feet against the lid.
*Better the Devil you know*
he says, and waves you on
with a warning.

Driving again, green fields
cringe into brown as you pass.
The Devil in your trunk is quiet now.
He knows you'll run out of gas
long before you get there
and the radio keeps playing
his songs.

# The Magician's Deathbed

*It's all in the gestures,*
he said, sleight of hand,
cards held behind his back.

That's the trouble with most
people, too much faith
in their eyes and ears,

too willing to smile away
the signs, their lives,
the empty box

where the girl hid,
then slipped out
the back hinge

but left a note
on the fridge
that she loved him.

# Notes and Acknowledgments

The following poems were adapted from an 1820 book of Pennsylvania Dutch Folk Magic, *Long Lost Friend* by John George Hohman:
"Spell To Settle Strife Among Relations"
"A Good Remedy for the Fever by a Long Lost Friend"

"Ouija" first appeared in the collection *Necessary Myths*, Broadkill River Press 2013

Versions of the some of the poems in this collection were first published in the following journals or websites:

*2River View:* "The Magician Dreams," "The Magician's Vacation"
*2 HawksQuarterly:* "A Good Remedy for Fever"
*American Poetry Review:* "Falling in Love with a Fiji Mermaid"
*Amaranth Review:* "For You, My Love, Alchemy"
*Apple Valley Review:* "Nova"
*Burnt District:* "Stalker"
*Chantwood Review:* "Supernatural," "Suburban Grimoire"
*Cheat River Review:* "Van Gogh's Sunflowers"
*Cleaver:* "The Magician Welcomes His Audience"
*Conclave:* "Ghosts," "Graduating from Magician School," "Sideshow Freaks at Lemon's Tavern"
*Concho River Review:* "Planting the Garden"
*Driftwood Press:* "SEO"
*Folio:* "The Magician Buys a Lottery Ticket"
*Gargoyle:* "Ode to a Jackalope"
*Mason's Road:* "Kabir Says"
*Moon City Review:* "Séance"
*Museum of Americana:* "Spell to Settle Strife Among Relations"
*One:* "More Advice for My Daughters"
*Painted Bride Quarterly:* "At the Occult Flea Market and Used Book Emporium"
*Phantom Drift:* "The History of Magic Part 1," "The Magician's Opening Act"
*Poetry City:* "Prodigal Satellite"
*Red Earth Review:* "Secrets of the Great Escape Artists"

*Schuylkill Valley Journal:* "Omens and Portents"
*Slipstream:* "Vanishing Point"
*Sow's Ear Poetry Review:* "Naming the Hurricanes"
*Sou'wester:* "Answer to Henri Cole's Green Shade"
*Storyscape Review:* "A Tarot Reading," "Idiots Guide to the Underworld"
*Superstition Review:* "The Good Lie," "Ode to Bats"
*Two-Hawks Quarterly:* "A Good Remedy for a Fever"
*U.S. 1 Worksheets:* "Between Two Fortune Tellers at the Midway"
*Vanish Magazine:* "The Magician's Handbook"